HERBERT HOOVER

The Presidents of the United States

George Washington
1789–1797

John Adams
1797–1801

Thomas Jefferson
1801–1809

James Madison
1809–1817

James Monroe
1817–1825

John Quincy Adams
1825–1829

Andrew Jackson
1829–1837

Martin Van Buren
1837–1841

William Henry Harrison
1841

John Tyler
1841–1845

James Polk
1845–1849

Zachary Taylor
1849–1850

Millard Fillmore
1850–1853

Franklin Pierce
1853–1857

James Buchanan
1857–1861

Abraham Lincoln
1861–1865

Andrew Johnson
1865–1869

Ulysses S. Grant
1869–1877

Rutherford B. Hayes
1877–1881

James Garfield
1881

Chester Arthur
1881–1885

Grover Cleveland
1885–1889

Benjamin Harrison
1889–1893

Grover Cleveland
1893–1897

William McKinley
1897–1901

Theodore Roosevelt
1901–1909

William H. Taft
1909–1913

Woodrow Wilson
1913–1921

Warren Harding
1921–1923

Calvin Coolidge
1923–1929

Herbert Hoover
1929–1933

Franklin D. Roosevelt
1933–1945

Harry Truman
1945–1953

Dwight Eisenhower
1953–1961

John F. Kennedy
1961–1963

Lyndon B. Johnson
1963–1969

Richard Nixon
1969–1974

Gerald Ford
1974–1977

Jimmy Carter
1977–1981

Ronald Reagan
1981–1989

George H. W. Bush
1989–1993

William J. Clinton
1993–2001

George W. Bush
2001–2009

Barack Obama
2009–

HERBERT HOOVER

DAVID C. KING

 **Marshall Cavendish**
Benchmark
New York

Marshall Cavendish Benchmark
99 White Plains Road
Tarrytown, NY 10591-5502
www.marshallcavendish.us

Library of Congress Cataloging-in-Publication Data

King, David C.
Herbert Hoover / by David C. King
p. cm. — (Presidents and their times)
Includes bibliographical references and index.
Summary: "Provides comprehensive information on President Herbert Hoover and places
him within his historical and cultural context. Also explored are the formative events of his
times and how he responded"—Provided by publisher.
ISBN 978-0-7614-3626-3
1. Hoover, Herbert, 1874–1964—Juvenile literature. 2. Presidents—United States—Biography—
Juvenile literature. 3. United States—Politics and government—1929–1933—Juvenile literature. I. Title.
E802.K56 2010
973.91'6092—dc22
[B]
2008038269

Editor: Christine Florie
Publisher: Michelle Bisson
Art Director: Anahid Hamparian
Series Designer: Alex Ferrari

Photo research by Connie Gardner

Cover photo by The Granger Collection

The photographs in this book are used by permission and through the courtesy of: *AP Photo:* 6, 13,
16, 68; *Corbis:* Bettmann, 9, 10, 17, 21, 23, 30, 32, 45, 48, 51, 56, 57, 71, 73, 82, 84, 86, 94, 98 (L);
Historical Standard, 37, 67, 89, 98 (R), Hulton Deutsch, 95, 99 (R); *Image Works:* Topham, 77;
Granger Collection: 3, 28, 34, 44, 53, 58, 63, 65, 85, 92, 97, 99 (L); *Art Resource:* Snark, 19, 80;
Getty Images: Hulton Archive, 27, 54; Popperfoto, 41.

Printed in Malaysia
1 3 5 6 4 2

CONTENTS

Herbert Hoover left the field of engineering to pursue a career in politics. Here, he appears in Tennessee during his electoral campaign in 1928.

THE EARLY YEARS

*H*erbert Hoover was one of the most famous and most admired men of the twentieth century. He grew up in modest circumstances in rural Iowa and then California. As a mining engineer he rapidly became wealthy in the American rags-to-riches tradition, traveling the world to locate deposits of oil, coal, iron ore, gold, and other minerals.

Having amassed a fortune of several million dollars, Hoover made a remarkable decision: he gave up his career in engineering in exchange for a life of public service. From 1914 on he accepted no salary for any of his work, including the presidency.

Hoover was a large man, standing just under six feet tall, with a broad, friendly face. He was exceptionally hardworking, often pushing himself to the point of exhaustion. People who knew him well found him to be amiable and knowledgeable, with a good sense of humor. But he was also extremely shy and uneasy in crowds, and he disliked the rough, often crude, behavior common in Congress. He was very demanding of himself and others. This made him stiff and unyielding, especially in a crisis.

And it was the crisis of the Great Depression that was Hoover's undoing. As the Republican nominee for president in 1928, he won an overwhelming victory over the Democratic candidate, Al Smith. A few months later, the stock market crash plunged the nation—and the world—into the worst economic crisis in history. Hoover worked tirelessly to find ways of lifting the nation out of it. But he could not bring himself to take the bold steps that were needed—steps that were later taken by the man who succeeded him, the Democrat Franklin D. Roosevelt.

A Quaker Childhood

Herbert Hoover was born on August 10, 1874, into a Quaker family in south central Iowa. He was the second of three children. The Quakers, also known as the Society of Friends, were generally pacifists—opposed to war and to any other violent solutions to conflict. There were exceptions; his father, Jesse, believed there were times when fighting was necessary. As a young man he had volunteered to serve in the Union army during the Civil War (1861–1865).

Hoover's mother, Hulda, was much stricter in her following of Quaker beliefs and was a well-known Quaker minister. She took part in many charitable activities and traveled through much of Iowa to speak at Quaker meetings.

In many ways Hoover's early years, spent in the small town of West Branch, were idyllic. As he wrote in his memoirs, he shared the "common experience of most Iowa children of my day in planting corn, hoeing gardens, learning to milk, sawing wood, and in the other proper and normal occupations for boys." His father was a successful and popular blacksmith. In 1877 he sold that business and opened a farm-equipment business.

There was plenty of time for fun, and West Branch offered many sources of enjoyment. Looking back years later, Hoover recalled some of those sources: "There was the swimming hole down by the railroad bridge," he remembered, and "there was Cook's Hill . . . where, on winter nights, we slid down at terrific speeds, with tummies tight to homemade sleds. . . . There are

Hoover grew up in this house in West Branch, Iowa.

also rabbits still being trapped . . . pigeons in this great forest, and prairie chickens in the hedges. . . . And in those days there were sun- and catfish to be had" using willow poles, butcher's string, and worms for bait.

One of the highlights of those early years was an eight-month period spent on the Osage Indian Reservation in Oklahoma (known then as Indian Territory), where his uncle Laban Miles was the government-appointed superintendent. From Osage friends Bert, as Hoover was then known, learned how to hunt with a bow and arrow and identify edible plants, as well as other woodland and prairie skills.

America was still in transition. The frontier was not fully settled, and a number of American-Indian societies were still fighting to hold onto their lands and ways of life. But the U.S. Army was slowly pushing them onto reservations—land set aside by the government for Indian tribes. By 1890 the fighting ended, and there was no longer any open frontier.

Bert's idyllic boyhood changed dramatically with the untimely death of his parents. On December 13, 1880, his father, Jesse, died of typhoid fever, at the age of thirty-four. His mother, Hulda, managed to keep the family together for the next three years. Tragedy struck again, however, when she caught a chill while walking home from a Quaker meeting in a neighboring town and the resulting chest cold turned into pneumonia. She died on February 24, 1883. She was thirty-five years old.

AN ORPHAN IN OREGON

With the death of both parents, it was necessary to split up the three Hoover children—Tad, the oldest, Bert, who was then ten, and Mary, nicknamed May. It was common for family members to take care of orphaned children, especially among the Quakers. Bert stayed with an aunt and uncle on their Iowa farm for a year, until another uncle asked for Bert.

Dr. John Minthorn and his wife, Laura, whose only son had died, lived in Oregon. Bert made the seven-day trip there in a wooden railroad car that was crowded with immigrants headed for the promised land of Oregon. It must have been a long and lonely journey for the boy. Naturally shy and quiet, the loss of his parents and the separation from his brother and sister led him to withdraw further into himself. His uncle and aunt also lived in a Quaker community, but one that was less strict than West Branch. Hoover's uncle liked to rephrase Quaker or biblical sayings, turning the meanings upside down: "Turn your cheek once," for example, "but if he smites thee again, then punch him."

Dr. Minthorn was strict and hardworking, and he expected hard work from his nephew. Bert had chores to do every day, which included feeding and watering the horses and chopping firewood. He often went with his uncle on long carriage rides to visit patients. Uncle Minthorn frequently used these occasions to lecture Hoover on physiology or American history, which proved useful in Bert's schooling.

Bert first attended the small local school where his Aunt Laura was principal. In 1885 he entered the Friends Pacific Academy in Newberg, where he was an average student but excelled in math. The motto over the academy's door expressed one of Uncle Minthorn's favorite sayings: "Whatsoever thy hand findeth to do, do it with all thy might." Whenever he had any free time, Bert made his way to the nearest fishing spot to indulge his great passion.

Bert's Uncle Minthorn displayed great generosity in many ways. In 1887, for example, he had Bert's older brother, Tad, come to live with them and then Bert's sister, May. A few months later the expanded family moved to Salem, Oregon, where Uncle

Hoover (far right) is photographed with his Sunday school class at Friends Pacific Academy.

Minthorn opened a real estate office. He also found time to build a house in which the three Hoover children could live with their grandmother.

Bert worked in his uncle's real estate office, where he learned to type. In the evenings he attended a small business college. Tad, having finished school, enrolled in William Penn College in Iowa, a

THE QUAKER INFLUENCE

Throughout Hoover's precollege years the Quaker religion was a constant part of his life. He was used to hearing people talk in antiquated speech, using archaic pronouns such as "thee" and "thou," just as he was accustomed to seeing—and wearing—plain and conservative clothes.

The Quaker religion focused on a close reading of the Bible and on "right" ways of behavior. By the time Hoover moved to Oregon, at age eleven, he had already read the Bible from cover to cover.

In his adult life, however, Hoover often didn't seem to be deeply influenced by his Quaker upbringing. Although he always wore a conservative dark suit, his behavior could seem decidedly un-Quaker. He liked to smoke an occasional cigar, for example, and he enjoyed a social drink, both activities frowned on by Quakers. But certain core Quaker values stayed with him, influencing his behavior and decisions—even when he wasn't aware of it. In his memoirs Hoover wrote, "The Friends have always held strongly to education, thrift, and individual enterprise. In consequence of plain living and hard work, poverty has never been their lot." He continued to hold to these values when he became president.

Quaker school; and the Minthorns urged Bert to attend a Quaker college as well. But Bert had already decided to study engineering, and no Quaker school offered an engineering program.

Two acquaintances helped Hoover find his direction. First, Robert Brown, a mining engineer, encouraged him to apply to Stanford, a new university in California. The Minthorns became convinced that Stanford was the right college for Bert when Dr. Joseph Swain, a well-known Stanford mathematics teacher, came to Salem to recruit students and give entrance exams. The fact that he was a Quaker was really all the Minthorns needed to hear.

College

Hoover was not a brilliant student in most subjects, so in 1891 he went to Palo Alto three months early for some tutoring that helped him meet Stanford's entrance requirements. In October he became part of Stanford's first class, later known as the "pioneer class."

During his college years Hoover was a large young man, standing about six feet in height, broad shouldered but not particularly muscular. His face was round and rather fleshy, topped with straight, unruly blond hair. He was extremely shy and walked with a slight slouch. He rarely spoke unless someone addressed him first, but he was always pleasant and had a good sense of humor.

Hoover was very ambitious and had tremendous stamina. He studied hard and, in his spare time, established a newspaper-delivery system and then a campus laundry. He was also paid thirty dollars a month for helping the chairman of the geology department. His summers were spent working with the U.S. Geological Survey, first in Arkansas, then in California. While gaining a solid knowledge of geology, Hoover managed to pay his way through Stanford without having to borrow money.

In spite of his shyness he was popular and became the class treasurer as well as the manager of the baseball and football teams. And he still indulged his love of the oudoors, going for hikes and, of course, fishing.

While at Stanford, Hoover (center, in suit) served as the manager of the football team.

In Hoover's senior year a young woman named Lou Henry enrolled in Stanford and became the first woman in the geology department. Lou was tall and athletic. Encouraged by her father, she developed a love for outdoor activities, especially hiking and fishing. Not surprisingly, Lou and Bert were a natural couple.

By the time Hoover graduated a year later, in 1895, with a degree in engineering, he and Lou knew they would someday marry. Hoover, however, had no money, no job, and no prospects, so he did not feel he could ask her to marry him. Lou understood him, and she was willing to wait.

Lou Henry worked in the chemistry lab at Stanford. Hoover and Henry married in 1899.

THE ADVENTURE BEGINS

In 1895, even with his degree in engineering, Hoover could not find work. Mining was not a sophisticated occupation, and the miners who worked with picks and shovels did not trust young men with college degrees. Therefore, Hoover decided to learn mining from the bottom up. At the Reward Gold Mine, outside Nevada City, California, he worked ten-hour days, pushing carts loaded with ore-bearing rocks, earning from $1.50 to $2.50 a day.

His first big break came when he was hired to do office work at the nearby Mayflower Mine, in San Francisco, by Louis Janin, one of the top experts on western mining. Janin was impressed with Hoover's eagerness to work and to learn, so he gave the young Stanford graduate every opportunity he could.

In 1896 Janin made Hoover the assistant manager of the Steeple Mine, in Carlisle, New Mexico, and later made him an investigator of installations for gravel mines in Colorado. In the autumn of 1896 Janin recommended Hoover to the great British mining company Bewick, Moreing and Company. They were looking for an American skilled in gold mining to work in western Australia. Hoover had the needed expertise and was offered the job in 1897.

Hoover was hesitant about accepting the position. He worried that he was too young and inexperienced. After all, the company was expecting someone in his mid-thirties, and Hoover was only twenty-two. To make himself look more mature, he

In order to learn about mining, Hoover took a job at a gold mine where he pushed carts loaded with ore much like this.

began growing the kind of beard he thought a rugged outdoors-man might have.

SUCCESS IN THE OUTBACK

In the spring of 1897 Hoover traveled east to New York, then sailed to London to meet his new employers—Bewick, Moreing and Company. By May he was in western Australia, taking a

Mining Engineering Comes of Age

Over the course of just twenty years Herbert Hoover became one of the most admired mining engineers in the world—and one of the wealthiest. Hoover was brilliant in his work, and he was fortunate to have entered the profession just as mining was becoming of great importance to almost every nation.

To understand the significance of mining engineering, consider the changes in industry and manufacturing that took place between 1850 and the early 1900s. The discovery of great oil deposits, for instance, came just in time to power newly developed industrial machinery and then motorized vehicles. Dozens of new industries emerged during these years, and many older ones grew much larger. Railroads grew with remarkable speed; between 1860 and 1900 five transcontinental lines were completed.

The harnessing of electricity also powered dozens of new industries, including those supplying telephones, electric railways, street and home lighting, and all sorts of tools and appliances. Each new industry, in turn, created the need for a host of new materials. The electrical industry, for instance, needed copper wiring, rubber insulation, steel turbines, and so on.

And that's where mining engineering came in. The task of the engineer was to search the earth's surface—and beneath it—for the veins and deposits of all those vital resources.

During this period mining engineers became globetrotters. Consider Herbert Hoover's career: in the space of a few years, he worked in several American states, then in Australia, China, Burma, Ethiopia, South Africa, Egypt, and Russia. He found one of the world's largest deposits of coal, as well as deposits of gold and silver.

train inland to Coolgardie. Once he arrived, he found that it was not an inviting place to work or live. Hoover said the Outback featured "red dust, black flies, and white heat." Coolgardie also featured fierce local whirlwinds called willie-willies, which could make life miserable. Even after the mining headquarters were moved to Kalgoorlie, Hoover didn't find conditions any more comfortable.

Hoover traveled in the blistering Outback heat on horseback, or sometimes by camel, which he said was "an even less

Hoover worked in Australia's Outback early in his mining career.

successful creation than a horse." His job was to survey and evaluate mines being offered to Bewick, Moreing and Company.

Hoover worked hard to find creative solutions to mining problems. When the lack of sufficient water halted the smelting of gold at one mine, Hoover found a filter press that recovered water for reuse. The lack of skilled miners on another occasion was addressed when he hired twenty Italian miners and encouraged other Italians to emigrate. Hoover managed to increase the mine's value, which gained him a promotion and a raise. He had already been receiving the princely salary of $7,500 a year plus expenses; that was increased to $10,000. The mine eventually produced $55 million in gold.

Hoover was still in his early twenties and was climbing rapidly up the ranks of mining engineers. He seemed to have an uncanny knack for locating mineral deposits. He was well liked by the miners—rough older men who overlooked his youth and called him Chief. They admired his extraordinary energy, although they worried about him when he worked himself to the point of exhaustion.

Hoover worked hard because he was ambitious and driven by his desire to succeed. Some people felt that while building his reputation, he didn't always give credit to those who helped him work out technical problems. He also had a tendency to exaggerate his own role in a given project, sometimes giving the impression that no one else was involved in the work. These criticisms were usually mild, but they troubled him throughout his life.

Following Hoover's success with the Australian mine, Bewick, Moreing and Company extended him a remarkable offer: go to China and direct *all* the mines owned by the Chinese

By the time he was in his mid-twenties, Hoover gained himself a strong reputation as a mining engineer.

government. Hoover immediately sent a cable to Lou Henry, explained the offer, and asked, "Will you marry me?" Lou sent a return cable of one word: "Yes!"

Lou and Bert were about to begin a twenty-year period of world travel. In an age before automobiles or air travel they circled the globe several times. In the process they started a family, and Hoover became both wealthy and famous.

TRAVELING CHINA AND THE WORLD

Three

*H*oover took a roundabout route from Australia to China, first traveling to the United States. He and Lou were married on February 10, 1899, at her parents' home in Monterey, California. They took a train to San Francisco in order to set sail the next day for China. They used the journey, which took nearly four weeks, to read about the culture, history, and language of China.

In March 1899 they arrived at the outskirts of Tientsin (now spelled Tianjin), at the mouth of the Pei-ho River. Hoover was to have a dual role in his new job: he was Bewick, Moreing and Company's representative in China and the resident chief engineer for the Celestial Bureau of Mines, as appointed by the Chinese government.

WELCOME TO THE REVOLUTION

Hoover's work in China was both profitable and difficult. He was troubled by the grinding poverty most of the people experienced, including those working in the mines, as well as the corruption and indifference of many Chinese officials.

Working with a large staff, including engineers he brought from Australia and the United States, he found China's greatest mineral wealth to be huge deposits of coal in the north of the country. He hoped to work out an arrangement with the government, headed by the young emperor Kuang-hsu. The emperor hoped to launch a period of reform and modernization in China, aided by Europe and the United States, even though he knew he would have to yield the control of some areas to the Westerners.

More conservative Chinese opposed the emperor's plan, fearing the loss of national sovereignty. They turned to the emperor's aunt, who had ruled as a **dowager** empress until her nephew was old enough to take the throne, for help. The dowager empress had the youthful emperor imprisoned, leading to an insurrection known as the Boxer Rebellion.

Years later Hoover wrote in his memoirs about the uprising that he and Lou lived through:

> *All [our] journeys were suddenly interrupted. There exploded in the faces of two twenty-six-year-old peaceful Americans [Lou and Herbert], an event that was to modify their lives, and also give them something to talk about for 'the rest of their born days. . . .' But, of far greater moment than that, it was to start one of the many currents which shaped the new century.*

When Hoover learned that the Boxers had targeted Peking and Tientsin, he rushed home to Tientsin to be with Lou. They thought their home would be safe until, Hoover reported, "Late one evening . . . a shell banged through a back window and then, exploding, blew out the front door and surroundings. Mrs. Hoover . . . was sitting in a side room playing solitaire. She never stopped the game."

During the uprising the Hoovers spent most of their time living in a compound that contained medical facilities with hundreds of other foreign families. About two thousand soldiers from several countries provided protection for the compound. At first the

China's dowager empress Tzu-Hsi supported the Boxers and their uprising in China in 1900.

Uprising in China

The Boxer Rebellion was an uprising by Chinese people who were eager to drive out all the "foreign devils" who, they felt, were taking over their country. In 1889 China's "boy emperor" Kuang-hsu had brought in great numbers of foreign experts to modernize China by bringing novel technology and business practices.

To the emperor's aunt, known as the dowager empress, and to many others, it seemed that foreign powers—England, France, Germany, Russia, and the United States—were rapidly dividing China into spheres of influence, considered de facto colonies, controlled by different countries.

To fight the foreigners, several secret societies were formed with names such as the Mailed Fist, the Plum Blossom Fists, and the Fist of Righteous Harmony. The "fist" images convinced foreigners that these were prizefighting organizations, so they called them the "Boxers."

According to reports, the Boxers slaughtered about 250 Christian missionaries and as many as 30,000 Christian converts in northern China. In early 1900 authorities learned that the Boxers' next targets were Peking and Tientsin. Thousands more Christians were slaughtered over the next few months. Peace was finally restored by the arrival of military contingents from Russia, Great Britain, and the United States.

families were safe, but then a large force of foreign-trained Chinese joined the Boxers, and for the next thirty days the bombardment of the city and the compound was almost constant.

Lou and Herbert became key figures in the defense of the compound. Lou looked after a dairy and spent most of her days working in one of the compound's hospitals. She always carried a revolver. "I took my turn as [captain of the guard]. . . . I could do it as well as the men. [But] Bert and I left the killing to the soldiers."

Hoover helped direct the construction of barricades made out of sacks of grain and sugar. He joined firefighting brigades

Lou Hoover inspects one of the large guns that shelled Tientsin during the rebellion.

and, on a bicycle, directed the carrying of food and water to about six hundred anti-Boxer Chinese soldiers. A classmate from Stanford who was there recalled, "Hoover was everywhere and everything to everybody [and appeared oblivious] to the constant shower of stray bullets." In many ways his actions were a preview of how he would work during World War I (1914–1918). Hoover also saved a number of leading Chinese, including a future premier, who had been suspected of aiding the Boxers; British troops were about to try them in a military court after executing some of their guards.

After a month of living in constant danger, they learned that American and Japanese troops were approaching the city. On July 15 the first U.S Marines arrived. The marine colonel decided to attack a nearby Boxer fortress and asked Hoover to guide the troops. Hoover agreed; and when marines on either side of him were shot, he asked for a gun, although he probably never used it.

The Boxer Rebellion quickly collapsed, and by August the Hoovers decided they had had enough of their China adventure. Tientsin was now in ruins, two-thirds of its buildings destroyed. Hoover estimated that during the fighting, he had seen some two thousand bodies floating down the Pei-ho River. "I was then 27 years old and delighted to get out of China into a larger engineering world." The Hoovers left China on a German mail boat, and they made it to London after traveling in stages for nearly two months.

Hoover's employers were delighted with Hoover's work—and grateful for it. Because of his efforts, they were able to form a British-based Chinese engineering company. Hoover received a partnership in Bewick, Moreing and Company, earning a salary of $12,500 a year, plus 20 percent of the profits. In addition, he was appointed the director of the Chinese company and received stock worth $250,000.

The Boxer Rebellion left Tientsin in ruin.

AROUND THE WORLD . . . FIVE TIMES

After doing more work in China, the Hoovers made London their
home base from 1902 to 1907. During that period the Hoovers
circled the globe five times. Their first son, Herbert Jr., was born

in 1903 in London. Within five weeks the baby, a nurse, and the Hoovers were on their way to Australia. By the time Herbert Jr. was a year old, he had been around the world twice.

The Hoovers' travels took about half of each year, and the rest of their time was spent in London. Traveling Americans enjoyed the Hoovers' hospitality, and the Hoovers' home became a hotspot for evening dinner parties and business discussions. While Bert was not outstanding in conversations, Lou was charming, intelligent, and capable of carrying on conversations on a wide variety of topics. She was devoted to Bert and put his career ahead of everything except their two sons (their second son, Allan, was born on July 17, 1907).

The Hoovers were not committed to England as their permanent home. In fact, in 1902 they built a small house in Monterey, California, with Lou's father. Five years later they built a small, six-room house in Palo Alto.

By 1908 Herbert was going his own way in business. He left Bewick, Moreing and Company and formed his own consulting firm. He soon had offices in London, San Francisco, New York, Paris, and Petrograd. He traveled with Lou, searching the world for mineral deposits. He also worked as a financier and promoter, striving to make poor mining operations profitable in exchange for a share of their profits.

The Hoovers' work took them to Australia, New Zealand, Japan, China again, Burma, South Africa, Egypt, and Russia. Herbert had his greatest success in Burma, where he developed a system for making the mining of zinc profitable. He did this at precisely the time that the demand for zinc was skyrocketing, as it was needed to produce the finest steel. He also found both silver

LOU HOOVER

Like her husband, Lou Henry was born in Iowa in 1874. Her family later moved to California. Her father, Charles D. Henry, a banker, encour-

aged her love of outdoor activities, such as hiking, camping, and fishing—activities that she and Bert shared throughout their lives.

In 1894 she entered Stanford University as the first and only female geology major. She met Bert the same year; and when he graduated the following year, they knew they would eventually marry, although Bert would not make a proposal until he had established his career and had been offered a job in China.

Lou graduated with a degree in geology, which enabled her to work in the field with Bert. In China she proved to be quite fearless during the Boxer Rebellion. She rode a bicycle on her daily rounds until the tires were shot away by stray bullets, forcing her to walk.

She also had an ear for languages. As a hobby, she and Bert spent several years translating a famous sixteenth-century treatise on mining and metallurgy from Latin into English. Lou also became proficient in Mandarin Chinese, and during the White House years she and Bert often conversed in Mandarin to prevent eavesdropping by members of the staff.

Throughout her life she not only supported Hoover but also was often an active participant in his affairs. During World War I, for example, she worked tirelessly on providing help for the Belgian people and, in 1919, was decorated by that country's King Albert.

While Hoover was serving as the secretary of commerce (1921–1929), Lou was the national president of the Girl Scouts. Later, as First Lady, she became famous for her frequent informal White House dinners, sometimes announcing them at the last minute. She always had a strong desire for a more normal home life. To that end she spent years planning their dream house overlooking the Stanford campus in Palo Alto, California. But she was also willing to accept the constant demands of public life.

Lou Hoover died suddenly of a heart attack in New York City on January 7, 1944. She was buried in Palo Alto but was then reinterred in West Branch, Iowa, next to her husband, following his death in 1964.

and gold deposits in Burma. There were many occasions when he lost money on a venture, but most of the time he was successful. By about 1914 his fortune was estimated at more than $4 million, a remarkable achievement at the time.

His reputation was known around the world by the time he was thirty years old. People referred to him as "young Hoover" or "the great engineer." A number of years later the American Institute of Mining Engineers named Hoover the "Engineer of the Century."

Hoover often overworked, pushing himself to the point of exhaustion. One of his biographers, David Burner, wrote, "His letters contain many references to exhaustion, both physical and mental. He placed himself under strains that would have broken ordinary men. But faced with the prospect of taking a vacation, he almost always drew back in panic or rushed through a sightseeing itinerary in breathtaking time."

By 1912 the war clouds were growing darker over Europe, and all the major countries were building up their armaments at a frantic pace. Hoover knew he could redouble his fortune by selling mineral resources to the Germans, British, French, Russians, and others. But because of his pacifist Quaker beliefs, the idea of profiting from war held no appeal for him.

The Hoovers decided it was time to go home to America. Lou made plans to enroll Herbert Jr. and Allan in school in California. The family was also ready to build their dream house on a spot they had selected overlooking the Stanford University campus.

Hoover seemed to be searching for a new direction, having reached a satisfactory plateau in his engineering career. He was becoming interested in education, perhaps teaching or, ideally,

becoming president of Stanford. He also was looking into buying a couple of newspapers as a means of influencing public opinion, mostly on issues of world peace.

His restless searching for a new direction stopped abruptly in the summer of 1914, when Europe exploded in the start of World War I. Without planning it, Hoover found himself on what he called "the slippery road of public life."

HUMANITARIAN HERO

Four

$\mathcal{T}$he Hoovers were in London when World War I erupted with frightening suddenness in August 1914. "I did not realize it at the moment," Hoover wrote later, "but on Monday, August 3 [1914], my engineering career was over forever."

AIDING STRANDED AMERICANS

The first task that required Hoover's unique skills was relayed in a message from the American ambassador to England, Walter Hines Page. The ambassador asked that the Hoovers aid the many American tourists trapped in England, plus those fleeing the European continent. In response, Hoover organized and directed the **American Citizens' Relief Committee**. Hoover was already known for his courageous work in China during the Boxer Rebellion, including his rescue of important individuals from China's government. Roughly 120,000 Americans sought assistance from Hoover's American Citizens' Relief Committee and its five hundred volunteers. Many of the people seeking assistance were holding foreign currency that had become useless and tickets to return home on German boat lines. Most needed steamship passage back to the United States. In addition, Hoover wrote, "Many of them only wanted to talk with somebody, somehow, somewhere about the approaching end of the world."

Lou Hoover also organized the Society of American Women in London, providing Americans in London with food, clothing, and lodging. She even arranged tours of London and the countryside to take the women's minds off the war and the delays in getting them back to America. In addition, Hoover's committee loaned stranded Americans more than $1 million; all but about $300 was repaid.

BELGIUM: FEEDING A NATION

When the war broke out, German forces marched across the Belgian border, violating the little country's neutrality in order to strike more swiftly at France. The Belgians chose to fight back, creating precious time for the Allies—England and France—to mobilize and prevent the Germans from taking Paris.

The Belgians paid dearly for their heroism. The Germans refused to provide food for the wartorn nation they were occupying. In fact, they took most of what was still being produced, and they prevented the importation of food by the civilians. By the end of August the people of Belgium were facing starvation. It was at this point that Hoover was asked to head the **Commission for Relief in Belgium** (CRB).

Belgium is a small country, but its population of 10 million made it the most crowded nation in Europe. Hoover's job was to find food for these people *every day* for however long the country was occupied by the Germans. He plunged into the work with great energy and enthusiasm. The challenge brought out his Quaker belief in helping those in need, especially those who were threatened by war.

Never before had the attempt been made to feed an entire nation. Hoover called it "the greatest job Americans have undertaken in the cause of humanity. . . . We are turning barren neutrality into something positive, a thing which has never been

Belgian women await free milk and food during Germany's occupation of their country during World War I.

done before. . . . [It would be] a monument in American history, the greatest charity the world has ever seen."

Hoover's wartime crusade would turn out to be the high point of his career. His array of skills were put to use and served him well. He worked with incredible energy, and his enthusiasm was infectious. When he refused to take a salary, for example, several others on his staff did the same. His great skill in organizing was another priceless asset—one that he had perfected when securing provisions for mines in remote or mountainous regions.

He had to find enough food to feed 11 million people (1 million were starving in northern France) *daily*. In addition, he needed the ships, railroads, trucks, and wagons—plus the workers—to load, unload, and distribute the food.

Money, too, was needed to pay for the provisions. Hoover proved to be a master at building sympathy for the Belgians and at raising funds. By 1915 it had become clear that the entire operation of the CRB, including the raising of funds, depended on him. The American ambassador to London reported:

> *The Commission for Relief in Belgium is Hoover and absolutely depends on Hoover who has personally made agreements with the Governments concerned and has carried these delicate negotiations through only because of his high character and standing and unusual ability. If he is driven to resign, the Commission will instantly fall to pieces. The governmental sources of money will dry up and the work will have to be abandoned.*

One other vital skill was Hoover's ability to persuade both sides in the fighting to let the supplies through the front lines. Germany, whose troops occupied Belgium, allowed the food to go to the people. On the Allied side, the British fleet had the entire coastline **blockaded**, and the British did not want the food falling into German hands. But they finally gave in to Hoover's requests.

All told, the Belgium relief program was a remarkable achievement. When the CRB was formed, no one thought its services would be needed for more than a year. They ended up being needed for four years, and the CRB collected 5 million tons of food and raised more than $1 billion.

Through it all Hoover avoided all forms of publicity. When a ceremony was held in Brussels, the Belgian capital, to honor him with a medal, for example, he simply didn't show up. He also tried to avoid photo sessions whenever possible. In a letter to President Woodrow Wilson, a leading diplomat wrote, "Life is worth more, too, for knowing Hoover. But for him Belgium would now be starving. . . . He is a simple, modest, energetic man who began his career in California and will end it in Heaven; and he doesn't want anybody's thanks."

"FOOD WILL WIN THE WAR"

On April 6, 1917, the U.S. Congress responded to the request of President Wilson by declaring war on Germany. Wilson then asked Hoover to come to Washington to take control of America's food organization, which involved increasing food production while reducing consumption during wartime. Lou and Bert immediately moved to Washington, and he was given the title of U.S. Food Administrator.

Hoover was determined to make this a voluntary program. He had acquired confidence in the willingness of people to work cooperatively, without the need for laws to force them to act. With Lou's help, he quickly set up a program. He called the program **conservation**; Americans called it "**Hooverizing**." He established "wheatless Wednesdays" and "meatless Mondays" as a way of reducing the demand for foods that were vital to the war effort.

There were several other steps in Hoover's program: posters and signs were hung throughout the country, making the campaign's slogan well known to everyone: "Food Will Win the War."

FOOD WILL WIN THE WAR
You came here seeking Freedom
You must now help to preserve it
WHEAT is needed for the allies
Waste nothing

As U.S. Food Administrator during World War I, Hoover created the "Food Will Win the War" campaign.

Booklets and newspaper articles offered advice on how to use less food while improving nutrition. With Hoover's "Food Will Win the War" campaign, the United States reduced consumption by 15 percent—without rationing. Creating guaranteed markets and prices for farmers' crops enabled the nation to triple its food exports.

Hoover's voluntary program was a great success. The Allied armies were kept well fed, and the United States built up a large surplus to prevent Europe from facing a postwar famine.

The United States hoped to remain neutral, but most Americans sympathized with the Allies. Anti-German sentiment increased when the Germans persisted in using submarine warfare. Submarines were one of several new weapons being used, and the Germans horrified the world by resorting to "unrestricted" submarine warfare—giving no warning to ships carrying civilian passengers and refusing to pick up shipwrecked survivors. The German High Command stopped the practice for a time but resumed it in a desperate effort to keep supplies hidden in civilian vessels

THE UNITED STATES AND WORLD WAR I

The major powers of Europe—Germany, the Austro-Hungarian Empire, England, and France—had been engaged in a massive arms race since the late nineteenth century. They had also formed tight military alliances: Germany and Austria-Hungary formed the Central Powers; the Allied powers were England and France. Smaller nations allied themselves on both sides.

from reaching England. The United States responded by declaring war on Germany in April 1917.

Europe had not witnessed a widespread war in a century—not since the Napoleonic Wars had ended in 1815. Consequently, the continent's rulers had little idea of what war would be like with the advent of modern weapons such as repeating rifles, machine guns, submarines, powerful cannons, tanks, and airplanes.

The result was a nightmare of violence and death—for civilian populations as well as the military. The fighting in western Europe settled into trench warfare—with both sides digging miles of trenches surrounded by barbed wire and filled with soldiers firing machine guns. Now and then one side or the other would be ordered "over the top," charging into the teeth of machine guns, barbed wire, and land mines, and sometimes through clouds of deadly mustard gas. Tens of thousands died, often without achieving any sort of advance.

Although American soldiers did not arrive in Europe in great numbers until the spring of 1918, their freshness and eagerness to fight was a great morale boost for the weary Allied soldiers. And the Americans fought well, helping force Germany to surrender in November 1918.

AID FOR POSTWAR EUROPE

When the war ended in November 1918, President Wilson sent Hoover to Europe to survey the food needs of the war-ravaged countries. Hoover's recommendations led to the creation of the **American Relief Administration** (ARA). For the next three years the United States was a major supplier of food to twenty-one countries in Europe and the Middle East.

The ARA was a nongovernmental agency that operated on the principle of compassion for all suffering people. Hoover insisted that this compassion be shown to the German people, even though French and British leaders felt that the defeated Germans should receive no aid. Hoover refused to give in, stating, "The United States is not at war with German infants."

The same conflict developed over providing aid to Russia following the Bolshevik/Communist Revolution of 1917. After years of fighting World War I (on the Allied side) and a civil war, thousands of Russians were starving every day in the early 1920s. Again, France and Great Britain, fearing a communist revolution, refused to approve aid for the Russian people. Again, Hoover ignored their wishes. In the middle of a meeting with all the Allies, he angrily banged his fist on the table and declared, "Twenty million people are starving. Whatever their politics, they shall be fed!"

In addition to his postwar relief work, Hoover was an adviser to President Wilson at the peace talks, held at Versailles, outside of Paris. Other Americans in the delegation were struck by how practical Hoover's advice was in contrast to Wilson's high-handed moral preaching. When Hoover was openly critical of Wilson's approach to the Treaty of Versailles and the League of Nations, he was dropped from the staff of presidential advisers.

Before returning to the United States, Hoover was treated as the war's greatest hero. Both individuals and governments cheered him and gave him award after award. In August 1919, just before returning to the United States, he visited Warsaw, Poland, where thousands of children, many of them barefoot, followed his motorcade, singing "The Star-Spangled Banner" and shouting his name.

At the end of World War I, Hoover headed the American Relief Administration, which provided food to many European countries.

Hoover responded in typical fashion; he ordered thousands of winter coats and as many pairs of shoes be given to the children.

Hoover was also hailed as a hero when he arrived in the United States. People referred to him as the "great engineer." At a time when the liberal wing of the Republican Party represented a **progressive** part of American politics, people were not sure to which party Hoover belonged. A diplomat in Wilson's Democratic administration gave an assessment of Hoover's character and political philosophy:

> *I think he is precisely the man that the **liberal** movement needs. . . . His hardness is all on the surface. He is a gentleman of rather wide culture . . . of a most democratic nature and with great human sympathies; his work in the [Belgian relief] Commission of course is one of the modern wonders of the world.*

As soon as he was home, however, Hoover did not want to think about where he fit in American politics. He wanted to get away from public life for a time.

SECRETARY OF COMMERCE

*I*n mid-1919 Herbert Hoover was back in Palo Alto with Lou and their two sons. The family had been together only on occasion over the previous five years. He finally had a chance to work with Lou on the actual construction of their dream house, overlooking the Stanford University campus.

Although the Hoovers enjoyed the restoration of their family life, Lou was not surprised when Bert was soon back in public life. Many people urged him to run for president in the 1920 election, but he did not feel ready for that. He did, however, state publicly that he was a Republican, and that led to his attaining his first governmental office.

THE "GREAT ENGINEER" IN GOVERNMENT

In the election of 1920 Republican Warren G. Harding was elected president. He invited Hoover to join his cabinet and asked him to choose between becoming secretary of commerce and secretary of the interior. Hoover chose commerce because he thought he could put more of his ideas into practice in that role.

Hoover served under Harding, and then under Harding's successor, President Calvin Coolidge, for a total of eight years—1921 to 1929. Secretary of commerce turned out to be the ideal position for Hoover. With his customary energy, he reorganized the Department of Commerce and transformed it into a service

Hoover was secretary of commerce in the administrations of Warren G. Harding and Calvin Coolidge (left).

organization designed to contribute to every aspect of the country's economy.

A central part of Hoover's political and economic philosophy was that a combination of **individualism** and cooperation was the key to America's economic future. "It is the essence of this democracy that progress [of the nation] must arise from progress of the individual."

In reorganizing the Department of Commerce, one of Hoover's main goals was to increase efficiency and eliminate waste. He tried to achieve the cooperation of businesses and individuals by offering them expert advice, information, and services. Instead of receiving endless publications detailing government regulations, businesspeople found bureaucrats who were eager to be of service.

Hoover's Department of Commerce found numerous ways to develop overseas markets for American products. Another major initiative was in **standardization**. For example, companies that manufactured nuts and bolts made the threads in different sizes, so buying replacements was a matter of confusion and frustration. With the help of the Department of Commerce, business executives discovered the savings that came with standardization. Soon there were standard sizes for everything from automobile tires to plumbing parts.

During his eight years as secretary of commerce Hoover made improvements in regulating navigation, irrigation, and electrical power. He encouraged the building of the Saint Lawrence Seaway as a way to link the Great Lakes with the Atlantic Ocean and the construction of Boulder Dam (later renamed Hoover Dam). He also improved the many bureaus associated with his department. These included the Bureau of the Census, the Bureaus of Fisheries and Lighthouses, and the Bureau of Standards, which dealt with the safety of things such as elevators and automobile brakes.

With the help of the Department of Commerce, U.S. manufacturers began standardizing their products.

Hoover took the lead in regulating the airways as radio developed in the 1920s. He encouraged local stations to join together in networks, creating NBC in 1926, then CBS. The new networks made money by selling advertising. He called an aviation conference to discuss codes and regulations for the emerging age of the airplane. He played a key role in developing the Air

Boulder Dam (later renamed Hoover Dam) was built with the encouragement of Herbert Hoover as a source of water for several states.

Commerce Act. In foreign affairs he supported the Dawes Plan, which eased the huge war debt owed by the German government. He knew that the continued decline of the German economy would have a devastating impact on the world; he also saw Germany as a potential defender against communism.

The Department of Commerce, which had previously been a disorganized collection of small bureaus, was soon humming with Hoover-style energy, with 1,600 employees on a crusade to modernize and expand the American economy. In a way the department represented the ideal of "progressive government"— a combination of private initiative, organized cooperation, and scientific management. Hoover held a number of well-publicized conferences, such as the one on aviation, that linked public and private action. He greatly expanded the role of government in the economy, but this was largely through cooperation rather than through new laws; and business leaders knew that the changes benefited them. These activities covered so many areas of economic life that people spoke of Hoover's "department of domestic affairs."

THE FLOOD OF 1927

In the spring of 1927 one of the most devastating floods in the nation's history smashed through the levees along the Mississippi River, flooding the region from Cairo, Illinois, to the Gulf of Mexico. More than one million people were driven from their homes, two million acres of cropland were destroyed, thousands of cattle were killed, and millions of dollars in damage was done to buildings and other property.

When floodwaters overran the Mississippi River in 1927, President Coolidge named Hoover the chairman of the Mississippi Flood Committee.

The governors of six states bordering the Mississippi River asked specifically to have Herbert Hoover help them deal with the emergency. President Coolidge responded by creating the Mississippi Flood Committee, with Hoover as the chairman and given complete control.

Hoover moved into the flood area with a virtual army of aid workers: a fleet of six hundred vessels, sixty government airplanes, hundreds of Red Cross nurses, thousands of National

On the orders of Herbert Hoover, members of the Salvation Army pack clothes to be shipped to areas afflicted by the flood.

THE "ROARING TWENTIES"

The decade of the 1920s was one of the most unusual periods in American history. It was a fast-paced age, with the automobile providing mobility people had never before experienced. Henry Ford's Model T led the way; 15 million of them had sold by 1927.

New inventions and advances in technology led to the production of a huge array of products for people to enjoy—radios, washing machines, refrigerators, and other appliances. Motion pictures were shown in elaborate "palaces" seating up to four thousand people. The first "talkies"—movies with sound—appeared in 1927.

Prohibition, America's "noble experiment" to outlaw alcohol, ended up creating a new form of entertainment—drinking at illegal "speakeasies" that acquired their "booze" from underworld figures such as the notorious Al Capone.

Many Americans were making enough money to enjoy this new age. They had enough leisure time, too, to make spectator sports popular for the first time. Huge crowds flocked to baseball parks, where larger-than-life heroes included Babe Ruth, who hit sixty home runs in 1927. Other great heroes emerged in every sport, such as Jack Dempsey in boxing, Red Grange in football, and Bobby Jones in golf. The greatest hero of all was Charles Lindbergh, a shy, handsome young man who made the first solo flight across the Atlantic Ocean, from New York to Paris.

Another popular "sport" was playing the stock market. Some people managed to make great sums in a short time, and the value of stocks seemed to be on a perpetual upward climb. Only a small percentage of Americans owned stocks, and fewer still were active buyers and sellers. But the market began to heat up when people started buying on margin—borrowing money in order to buy stock, hoping to pay what they owed to the broker and still make a profit. As stock prices continued to soar, the market became overheated. If all the brokers had to call in their outstanding loans, the whole system would collapse. But until 1929, Americans enjoyed the ride.

Guardsmen, army engineers, weather bureaus, and thousands more volunteers. Hoover set up headquarters on a bluff above the river and made frequent tours of the flooded area in a private railroad car. He called the flood "the greatest peace-time calamity in the history of the country."

During the relief work Hoover discovered ways to improve the health of rural people living in the South. Aided by a grant from the Rockefeller Foundation, he established one hundred health units to work in the stricken area for a year. By improving living standards, the health workers were able to reduce the incidence of malaria, typhoid, and pellagra.

Herbert Hoover was well known before the flood relief, but his work in this emergency raised his fame to new heights. One of his biographers, David Burner, concluded, "In the spring of 1927, the Commerce Secretary dominated the headlines in a drama restating all the best that he represented of the engineer, the humanitarian, and the administrator." Referring to the approaching 1928 election, Burner added, "The great Mississippi flood ruined the South . . . and elected Hoover."

Helping Children

Both Herbert and Lou Hoover devoted time and energy to serving children. Lou had long been active in the Girl Scouts. She had served as president of the national organization and remained a board member even while carrying out her responsibilities as the wife of a cabinet officer.

Bert became president of the American Child Health Organization, and he raised funds to promote health education in communities and schools. He also formulated the Child's Bill of

Rights to encourage helping children through parental guidance, as well as immunization and vaccination programs. In addition, he helped launch a program to distribute milk and hot lunches to students attending schools in poor areas. These programs added to the public's awareness of his accomplishments.

A PERIOD OF PROGRESS

Six

*I*n 1928 President Coolidge made it clear that he did not want to run for another term as president. His office was immediately flooded with letters and telegrams urging him to seek the Republican nomination. With the nation's economy apparently still growing at a healthy rate, it seemed an ideal time for the most progressive Republican to serve the nation in new ways. Hoover easily won the party's nomination.

THE 1928 CAMPAIGN

The 1928 presidential election campaign was a study in contrasts. The Democrats nominated Alfred E. Smith, governor of New York, the first Catholic to run for the presidency. The two men agreed on several issues, including the reform of child welfare programs, the modernization of business practices, oil conservation, and the development of water resources.

There were also major differences. Smith favored a farm program that would fix agricultural prices and flood foreign markets with surplus American products. He campaigned hardest for repeal of the Prohibition Amendment. Hoover did not think Prohibition belonged in the Constitution, but because it was already there, he believed the ban on alcohol should be enforced.

The thing that diminished Smith's chances of winning the election, apart from the prosperity for which people credited

ANTI-CATHOLIC SENTIMENT AND THE KLAN

One of the dramatic changes Americans experienced in the early years of the twentieth century was a huge influx of immigrants, especially from eastern and southern Europe. Many native-born Americans were upset by this wave of new residents. The newcomers spoke unfamiliar languages—Greek, Italian, Polish, and Russian. Many were members of the Jewish faith, and even greater numbers were Catholics.

In small towns across America people felt that their traditions and values were being threatened. One response to the fear was the rebirth of the Ku Klux Klan (KKK). The Klan had been formed as a social organization by Confederate veterans after the Civil War, but it quickly became a means of intimidating freed slaves. It was disbanded before the end of the nineteenth century but was then revived in Georgia in the early 1920s. It welcomed members who were antiforeign, anti-Catholic, anti-Semitic (Jewish), antiblack, and antiurban.

The KKK grew quickly, and by the early 1920s it was blamed for dozens of floggings as well as several murders and kidnappings. By the mid-1920s its membership had reached more than 4 million.

The Klan declined quite suddenly in the mid-1920s, when an Indiana Klan leader was found guilty in a sordid case of kidnapping, rape, and murder. There was a partial recovery in 1928, when the Democrats nominated Al Smith for the presidency. There is no way to measure how much Smith was harmed by anti-Catholic sentiment in the 1928 election, largely because voters credited the Republican Party with the nation's continuing prosperity. The strong anti-Catholic prejudice lingered long after the 1920s and after the decline of the KKK.

the Republicans, was his Catholic faith. Many Americans, especially in the South, distrusted Catholics; and some said the church and the pope would influence the U.S. government.

Hoover's greatest weakness as a campaigner was his extraordinary shyness. He could speak comfortably in small groups but giving a speech to a large audience was nearly impossible for him. His voice became a tiresome monotone, and he rarely looked up from his prepared notes. Henry Pringle, a journalist and historian, described Hoover's public-speaking style this way:

> One hand is kept in his pocket, usually jingling coins or keys placed there to ease his nerves. He has not a single gesture. . . . He reads— his chin down against his shirt front—rapidly and quite without expression. . . . He can utter a striking phrase in so prosaic, so uninspired and so mumbling a fashion that it is completely lost on nine out of ten of his [listeners].

The coming of age of radio helped Hoover to some extent. He could reach millions of people while standing or sitting comfortably in front of a microphone. Unfortunately, the radio did not improve the quality of his speeches. Al Smith was just the opposite as a speaker and a campaigner. He loved to travel and meet people.

In the end the nation's prosperity was the key to the election. People felt that Hoover's technical skills and his combination of individualism and cooperation would help build an even brighter future. Hoover won in one of the greatest landslides achieved by a Republican. The popular vote was 21 million for Hoover, 15 million

Herbert Hoover addresses a crowd in New York during his campaign for the presidency.

for Smith. In the electoral vote Hoover carried 40 states, with 444 electoral votes, to Smith's 8 states, with 87 votes. Hoover's vice president was Charles Curtis.

President Herbert Hoover and vice president Charles Curtis, along with their wives, are photographed on March 4, 1929, the day of Hoover's inauguration.

THE HOPEFUL BEGINNING

The Hoovers began their White House tenure in March 1929 with a spirit of cautious optimism. Hoover felt that while serving as president, he could implement ideas that would build an even brighter future for the nation.

At the same time he wondered if he was as great a man as people of the time seemed to think. Shortly before his inauguration as the thirty-first president, Hoover made this remarkably prophetic statement:

> My friends have made the American people think me a sort of superman, able to cope successfully with the most difficult and complicated problems. . . . They expect the impossible of me and should there arise conditions with which the political machinery is unable to cope, I will be the one to suffer. . . . I would be sacrificed to the unreasoning disappointment of a people who expected too much.

Lou Hoover, as always, shared every moment with her husband, the bad as well as the good. To her, the presidency was one more of their "adventures." To make their new living quarters more comfortable, she transformed the Lincoln study from a bedroom into an office for her husband. She bought more comfortable furniture, often using her own money. She even made it possible for their youngest son, Allan, to live with them after his 1929 graduation from Stanford by finding living quarters for his pet alligator.

The First Lady was at her best when entertaining a diverse array of guests. She arranged frequent luncheons as well as elegant dinner parties. She also continued to enjoy getting away, especially outdoors. Under her supervision a presidential retreat was built at the headwaters of the Rapidan River in the Blue Ridge Mountains. When Hoover left office in 1933, he donated Camp Rapidan to the government.

Hoover's Achievements

Herbert Hoover's presidency is so strongly associated with the nightmare of the Great Depression that little is remembered of his accomplishments. After eight years of conservative Republican presidents, Hoover's administration represented the party's progressive wing, eager for change.

One of his first steps was to warn wealthy business owners that he intended to end the preferential treatment they had enjoyed during the Harding-Coolidge years. During his first week in office he stated publicly that "excessive fortunes are a menace to true liberty by the accumulation and inheritance of economic power." He almost immediately took steps that discouraged the Republican leaders who had long maintained close ties with business. He took steps to improve civil liberties, and he set limits on oil drilling on governmental lands.

Other steps taken by Hoover involved trying to improve race relations. During his tenure as secretary of commerce, the Hoovers had refused to sign a neighborhood agreement to keep "Negroes and Jews" from buying, renting, or leasing property on their street. In May 1929, barely two months after his inauguration, Hoover invited Robert Moton of the Tuskegee Institute to the White House, duplicating a gesture made thirty years earlier when President Theodore Roosevelt invited Booker T. Washington to the White House. Hoover's more concrete actions included increasing the number of black Americans in federal employment to 54,684 by the end of his term. He appointed more African Americans to middle positions than did Harding and Coolidge combined. He also increased funding for Howard University and the Freedmen's Hospital, two all-black institutions.

THE FEDERAL FARM BOARD

One of the major problems faced by America's farmers was surplus—an overabundance of one or more crops. The surplus occurred when every farm harvested and marketed a crop at the same time. This was especially true in good crop years. When wheat, corn, or any other crop was harvested and placed on the market, the price plummeted—and so did farm families' incomes. If some of the crop could be held back and sold later, this would keep the price up.

(continued)

Keeping crop prices stable was the idea behind the Agricultural Marketing Act, passed by Congress in 1929. The measure created an eight-member Federal Farm Board, which had a $500 million revolving fund to use for storing, buying, or selling products in order to raise the price, and therefore the income, of the farmers. This was probably Hoover's most progressive move—a change that sent the country in new directions.

In some ways the Federal Farm Board was a prelude to the New Deal program that supported the price of agricultural products. A major difference was that the New Deal's price supports were paid by the government, while the Hoover program was voluntary.

During the early months of the Depression the Federal Farm Board managed to stabilize prices for cotton and wheat; it also helped stabilize the prices of corn, grapes, citrus fruits, dairy products, and a few other farm commodities. By 1932 huge surpluses of cotton and grains were in storage. The board managed to distribute much of the surplus to the needy through the Red Cross. But it could not manage the enormous surpluses that continued to pile up as the Depression deepened and a growing number of families lost their farms.

In addition, Hoover hoped to launch a nongovernmental approach to aiding both black and white tenant farmers, called sharecroppers. He planned to have private foundations provide funds that would enable tenant farmers to buy the land they worked. It was a bold scheme, but the coming of the Depression made it impossible to execute.

Many of Hoover's reform ideas reflected the Quaker philosophy, including prison reform. The president took major steps to improve prisons and to reduce the overcrowding caused by people convicted of Prohibition-era crimes. New penitentiaries were built that included schools for training guards and provisions for

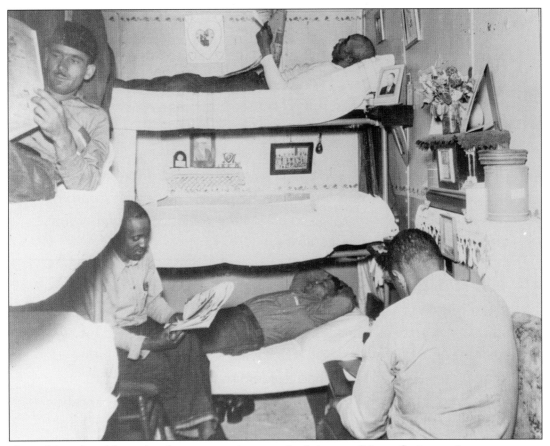

One of President Hoover's reforms was to improve the living conditions of prisoners in state penitentiaries.

allowing convicts to work outside the prison walls. Schooling was made available to inmates, and the Public Health Service provided them with better health care.

Another success was the creation of the White House Conference on Child Health and Protection. Using surplus funds from the Belgian relief program of 1914, the 1930 conference involved more than 2,500 delegates. The group developed a report on child welfare that provided more information than has any conference before or since.

The Hoover administration also took important steps to improve conditions for American Indians. Hoover believed in preserving Indian culture, making no distinction between tribal and individual achievements. He dismissed an insensitive commissioner of Indian affairs and named two prominent Quakers as commissioner and assistant commissioner, knowing the Quaker belief in fair treatment. Hoover also took steps to improve education while reducing enrollment in the unpopular Indian boarding schools, whose mission was to assimilate American-Indian youth into European-American culture.

TOO MUCH OPTIMISM?

From March to October 1929 Hoover seemed to be enjoying the start of his term as president, going about his duties with his typical energy. He constantly displayed that array of interests, knowledge, and skills that had made him famous earlier.

Even before his inauguration, however, Hoover showed signs of overconfidence in the nation's prosperity and in the ability of his administration to make even greater progress. In August 1928, when he accepted his party's nomination, Hoover stated,

"We in America today are nearer to the final triumph over poverty than ever before in the history of any land. The poorhouse is vanishing from among us."

Before long, those words would come back to haunt him. Within eight months of taking office, the stock market crashed, heralding the start of the Great Depression. In that era people's dreams of prosperity were replaced by hunger and fear.

THE DEPRESSION YEARS

$\mathcal{A}$fter Hoover's election there was a frenzy of stock buying. People were so confident in the new administration that they were willing to borrow money and buy stocks on margin. Banks were also gambling in this way, even using depositors' money; and there were no laws to prevent them.

Hoover tried to stop the runaway speculation, but no one paid any attention. He urged Congress, the banks, and New York governor Franklin D. Roosevelt to establish rules to stop the practice; but nothing was done. Furthermore, farm prices were steadily declining because of surpluses. Corporate profits remained high but wages did not, so people's purchasing power was also declining.

THE STOCK MARKET COLLAPSE

On October 30, 1929, *The New York Times* reported:

> *Stock prices virtually collapsed yesterday, swept downward with gigantic losses in the most disastrous trading day in the stock market's history. Billions of dollars in open market values were wiped out as prices crumbled under the pressure [to liquidate] securities which had to be sold at any price.*

The prices of stocks that had sold for $30, $40, or $50 per share fell to pennies. Thousands of investors lost fortunes; hundreds of businesses and banks were wiped out. It was an economic crisis on a scale never before seen in America.

Most leaders of the Republican Party believed that there was nothing the government could do to prop up the stock market. This was part of the usual business cycle, they said, and in time the market would rebound and start another upward climb.

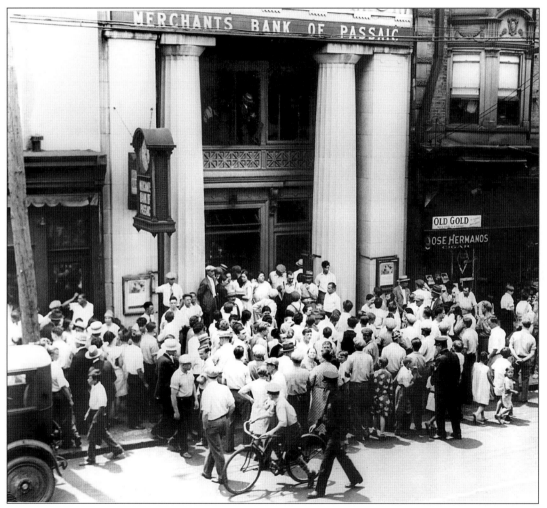

Depositors crowd in front of a New Jersey bank following the crash of Wall Street.

Hoover did not agree. He immediately called business leaders to the White House, where he asked them not to lay off workers or cut wages. He told them it was not fair to have labor bear the cost of the sagging economy. He also warned the business leaders that this economic crisis was likely to be more serious than any previous downturn. "No one," he said, "can measure the problem before us or the depth of the disaster."

Another part of Hoover's recovery plan was to urge state and local governments to join private charities in helping people made destitute by the crisis. In addition, he asked Congress to appropriate funds for **public works** that would expand employment on a few government-run projects.

Although Hoover would soon be condemned for doing nothing about the economic crisis, it's clear that he did have a plan; and many Americans assumed the steps he had taken would lead to recovery. The president, in fact, was more active than any of his predecessors had been in dealing with an economic crisis.

FROM CRASH TO GREAT DEPRESSION

The stock market crash did not cause the Great Depression, but the two crises were related. The stock market losses wiped out the fortunes of many people who could have been involved in business expansion. Those who lost their money in the market were also the men and women who were able to buy the most luxury products. As these people reduced or stopped their spending, American and European businesses reduced production, and workers were laid off.

Another major reason the Depression hit the depths it did was that factory production in the Coolidge years did not represent healthy growth. People could buy only so many automobiles, refrigerators, radios, or houses. In addition, many of these things had been purchased on credit, and paying off those loans reduced families' purchasing power. People who did have jobs and a little extra money became afraid to spend it. With spending reduced more and more, factories laid off more workers, and a growing number of businesses failed.

Increases in import duties (tariffs) added to the economic troubles. Farmers, who counted on the sale of crops or animals to survive, experienced a dramatic drop in prices at this time. Europe, still reeling from the destruction caused by World War I, had a low standard of living at the time. The availability of land and cheap labor allowed European nations to export agricultural products at low prices. As these products flooded the market, prices dropped so low that American farmers plowed crops under or killed cattle or sheep rather than sell them at a loss.

In 1930 Hoover reluctantly signed a bill called the Hawley-Smoot Tariff, which he hoped would protect farmers by placing import duties on products coming into the country. Instead, the measure touched off a tariff war, sending every country's tariffs to record highs. This further reduced demand for U.S. goods.

For a few months in 1930 there were signs of recovery, but business owners, feeling pinched, ignored Hoover's plea and began laying off more workers. The number of unemployed Americans, which was 1.5 million at the time of the crash, had jumped above 4 million in 1930. And that was just the beginning. By 1933, when the Great Depression was at its worst, more than 13 million were unemployed—almost one-third of the labor force.

Men crowd an employment agency seeking work during the early 1930s.

Even people with jobs often had their wages reduced. Historian Jeane Westin describes the situation for some women:

> *Women office workers in New York who previously earned forty-five dollars a week were now taking home only sixteen dollars. . . . And black women in Alabama, working twelve-hour, six-day weeks in steamy laundries, made a pitiful $5.85 a week.*

President Hoover tried hard to boost people's spirits, usually by assuring them that the Depression would soon be over. In June 1930, for example, a delegation of citizens came to the White House to urge him to make a large increase in public works funds to provide jobs for the unemployed. The president told them that such a step was not necessary. "Gentlemen," he said, "you have come six months too late. The Depression is already over."

History has shown that Hoover was completely wrong. His greatest weakness was his inability to understand how deep the Depression could get or how long it could last. The economic chaos involved all of the world's nations. Countries that had borrowed heavily from U.S. sources could no longer make payments on those loans, further harming the U.S. economy.

THE DEPTHS

By 1932 and 1933 the Depression reached its lowest point, with one-third of the workforce jobless and many of the rest working reduced hours. When people hit bottom, there was nowhere to turn—unemployment benefits did not exist, nor did health insurance, welfare, or social security. A family might get a small amount of help from public charities or churches, but these sources were low on funds, except for the small amounts still available to run soup kitchens.

Historian Robert Goldston described the growing sense of despair and humiliation:

During the spring of 1930 bread lines began to appear . . . long lines of patient, humiliated men shuffling forward slowly to receive a bowl of watery soup and a crust of bread from charity kitchens,

In 1932 the needy form a breadline on the streets of New York City.

Salvation Army halls, and local relief agencies. . . . You might go to the local poorhouse, your children to an orphanage. . . . You racked your brain to find out . . . what sin you committed to earn such terrible punishment.

By 1933 an estimated 200,000 teenagers, mostly boys, roamed the nation's roads and railroad lines. They joined the many adults who had no jobs and no homes. During a Congressional hearing one Oklahoma resident testified as early as 1932 that "the roads of the West and Southwest teem with hungry hitchhikers. The campfires of the homeless are seen along every railroad track. I saw men, women and children walking over the hard roads." Within three years of the stock market crash, five thousand banks had failed, wiping out the savings accounts of about 9 million people. During that period an average of 100,000 jobs were lost each week.

The American people were increasingly confused and frightened by what was happening. They had always believed that working hard and saving money were the keys to prosperity. But that simple formula no longer held true. Instead, they felt themselves being moved by powerful forces they could neither understand nor control.

In the past people with land could always grow some crops or raise a few animals to help them through a hard year. But a severe drought in 1930 and 1931 made that impossible in large areas of the country.

The worst of the farm crisis was yet to come. In the mid-1930s the Great Plains region was struck by devastating dust storms. Overfarming and drought transformed thousands of acres of prime farmland into dry, dusty fields. Winds blew away the fertile topsoil from the farmland, as there was little vegetation in place to hold onto it. Nearly 3 million people lost their land and their farms. Many people, who came to be called "Okies," joined

A farmstead lies abandoned in Oklahoma during the 1937 dust bowl.

the migration west to California, where conditions were better, but not by much.

THE ENEMY IN THE WHITE HOUSE

When the hoped-for recovery did not take place, people's misery turned to resentment and anger. The most obvious target for their anger was President Hoover. The man who was hailed as the great humanitarian of the twentieth century was now criticized as the man who did too little to pull the country out of the Depression—a president who did not seem to care about the nation's people.

Month after month the criticisms became increasingly bitter. During the 1928 election campaign the Republican Party had promised voters "two chickens in every pot and a car in every garage." Hoover himself had said that America was close to eliminating poverty. And despite the conditions present during the Depression, he maintained that optimism. He told a group of White House visitors, for example, "We have come out of each previous depression into a period of prosperity greater than ever before. We shall do so this time."

A political cartoon satirizes Hoover's efforts to cope with the Depression.

Such statements and slogans were continually hurled back at Hoover and his administration. State and local officials, along with a growing number of people, urged the president to provide direct aid to the millions of destitute, many of whom were reduced to picking scraps out of garbage dumps. But Hoover felt he had to refuse. He believed strongly that giving direct aid to people—called a **dole**—would sap people's will to work, making them dependent on government handouts.

Besides, he said, "Prosperity cannot be restored by raids on the public treasury."

People who had lost everything often ended up in shanty-towns, living in shacks made of cardboard and scrap tin. They called these makeshift hovels "Hoovervilles." The newspapers they stuffed into their clothes for warmth were called "Hoover blankets." Hoover's beliefs in individualism and voluntary action now turned back on him as taunts.

Many who lost their life savings wound up in shantytowns nicknamed Hoovervilles, like this one in Seattle, Washington.

As Americans began feeling that Hoover didn't care what happened to them, some critics began to blame him for the economic hardships, saying that he actually caused the Depression. The criticisms sometimes took the form of biting humor. A radio humorist, for example, had one comic say, "There's been a big rise in the stock market." "Oh?" the other replies, "Did Hoover die?" Humorist Will Rogers offered this: A man bit into an apple and found a worm. "Damn that Hoover," the man said. And when Hoover was given a twenty-one-gun salute in West Virginia, a man said, "Gosh, every shot missed him!"

Hoover was deeply hurt by the criticism. He was doing his best and following the principles that had guided him so well through all his years of public service. The White House usher, Ike Hoover (no relation), recalled, "There was always a frown on his face and a look of worry."

HOOVER'S FEDERAL RESPONSE

In July 1932 President Hoover finally yielded to the ever-increasing pressure to provide more assistance to the people. He went against his instincts to approve the **Reconstruction Finance Corporation** (RFC). The RFC was authorized to make 1.5 million dollars available for public works and 3 million dollars available for loans to states. These were small amounts. In Pennsylvania, for example, the state's loan allowed a jobless worker $0.11 a day for food.

Passing the RFC was a bold step for Hoover, and it was considered one of the best ways to ease the Depression. The problem was that Hoover did not use the RFC with the kind of energy that was required. He also failed to use some of the funds for well-publicized programs, which would have showed the nation how deeply he did care. Instead, the men who managed the fund never used all of the money; and what they did use, they gave to large banks and railroads. This was helpful to a few giant corporations, but it did little to stimulate economic growth.

Despite its shortcomings, Hoover's RFC served as a model for Franklin Roosevelt's New Deal. In fact, the New Deal continued and expanded the RFC.

THE BONUS MARCH OF 1932

In 1924 Congress voted to award bonuses to the veterans of World War I, to be paid in 1945. In May 1932 about 15,000 veterans marched into Washington and set up camp near the Capitol. When their request for immediate payment was turned down by Congress, many veterans left; but thousands remained in their rather squalid camp, which began to look like a typical Hooverville.

In July Hoover ordered that the camp be cleared. General Douglas MacArthur, aided by Major Dwight D. Eisenhower, led a cavalry regiment with drawn sabers and an infantry regiment with fixed bayonets and tear gas bombs, plus six tanks. It did not take long for this force to drive out the veterans and burn down their shacks.

Any credit the Hoover administration had been given in the eyes of the people for creating the RFC was wiped away by the excessive force used against the Bonus Army. It did not matter that it was MacArthur who had exceeded his authority in the use of force. What remained in people's minds was the image of a heartless president who used the army to crush a peaceful protest by men who had fought for their country.

Members of the Bonus Army make camp in Washington, D.C., seeking bonus payment for their participation in World War I.

A few months later the election of 1932 pitted Democrat Franklin D. Roosevelt against Hoover, who had reluctantly been nominated by the Republican Party. Hoover knew he had little chance of winning, but he was deeply hurt by the personal attacks leveled against him by Roosevelt and the Democrats. In his memoirs Hoover wrote, "The major strategy of the opposition was to attach to me, personally, the responsibility for the worldwide depression and its evils."

The election went as expected, with the popular, cheerful Roosevelt winning 23 million popular and 472 electoral votes to Hoover's nearly 16 million popular and 59 electoral votes. In March 1933 Lou Hoover did her best to cheer up her disheartened husband as they left Washington for their home in Palo Alto, California.

The Later Years

After the stormy years spent in the White House, the Hoovers were relieved to be back in their Palo Alto home. For the next thirty years, however, Hoover didn't reduce his activity level much.

World Affairs Issues

One of Hoover's major projects was building the Institution on War, Revolution and Peace, which he had started in 1919. He had said he wanted to collect library material on war in general. He eventually brought together important documents on the eras of World Wars I and II from British, Chinese, German, and Soviet sources. The institution became one of the largest manuscript libraries in the world. In 1941 the Hoover Tower was dedicated on the Stanford campus to house the collection.

Hoover tried to keep in touch with events by reading as many as thirty newspapers that were delivered to Palo Alto every day, but he didn't like being so far from the center of politics. As a result the Hoovers began spending most of each year in a suite at the Waldorf-Astoria Hotel in New York City.

Hoover also devoted a good deal of energy and time to the Boys Clubs of America. Through his activities the organization grew from 140 chapters to more than 600.

Hoover vs. Roosevelt

Throughout the 1930s Hoover remained highly critical of President Roosevelt and his New Deal policies. He was bitter at

Mar. 4, 1933 THE | Price 15 cents

NEW YORKER

Peter Arno

This unpublished New Yorker *cover from 1933 depicts a grim Herbert Hoover and a smiling Franklin Delano Roosevelt on the way to his inauguration.*

seeing many of his own ideas and fledgling projects carried to fulfillment and hailed as examples of Roosevelt's brilliance. He also resented that many New Deal policies involved social engineering directed by the government rather than the volunteerism that Hoover believed in so strongly. He vented his criticisms in two publications: *The Challenge to Liberty* (1934) and a volume in his collection *Addresses Upon the American Road* (1938), which dealt with the years 1933 to 1938.

Hoover was also critical of Roosevelt's foreign policy. He felt that Roosevelt was too aggressive in threatening intervention against Nazi Germany and militarist Japan. He was convinced that Roosevelt was leading the nation into war. He much preferred following the Stimson Doctrine, a highly regarded statement from Hoover's secretary of state that said simply that the United States would not recognize any territory acquired by force.

When Japan attacked Pearl Harbor on December 7, 1941, however, Hoover supported the war effort with enthusiasm. But he did not agree with dropping the atomic bombs in 1945. "The use of the Atomic bomb . . . revolts me," he wrote to a friend. "The only difference between this and the use of poison gas is the fear of retaliation. We alone have the bomb."

Earlier, in January 1944, Lou Hoover had died suddenly of a heart attack in their New York hotel suite. She was sixty-eight years old. Her last appearance in the news had been in 1933, when she broke precedent by showing Mrs. Roosevelt around the White House.

POSTWAR RELIEF . . . AGAIN

When World War II ended in 1945, President Harry Truman asked Hoover to make a survey of world food needs following the tremendous destruction caused by the war. Hoover made a whirlwind tour of twenty-five countries, covering 35,000 miles in fifty-seven days. The government acted on his recommendations, and the risk of famine was averted by 1946.

After World War I Germany had been forced to take the blame for starting the conflict and also had to pay **reparations** to England and France. The resulting debt was far too large for Germany to pay, and the resulting collapse of that nation's economy was a major reason that the Great Depression became a worldwide phenomenon.

In his report on forestalling a global food crisis, Hoover recommended taking steps that would enable Germany to have a strong and independent economy. His suggestions in 1947 led to the rebuilding of Germany. German chancellor Konrad Adenauer showed his appreciation when, on his first visit to the

Hoover tours Poland in 1946 in an effort to study the effect of the war and the shortage of food in war torn Europe.

United States, in 1953, his first stop was Hoover's Waldorf-Astoria suite.

FINAL PUBLIC SERVICE

During the postwar years Hoover spent much of his time writing and concluding two public-service projects involving the modernization of the government. In 1947 Congress authorized the creation of a Commission on Organization of the Executive Branch of the Government. President Truman asked Hoover to serve as its chairman, and it became known as the Hoover Commission. Doing this work had been one of Hoover's dreams since his early days in government. Most of his commission's recommendations were adopted, saving the government several billion dollars.

In his final years of service, Hoover served as the chairman of the Committee on Organization of the Executive Branch of the Government during the presidency of Harry Truman.

A second Hoover Commission was established by President Eisenhower when Hoover was eighty years old. This work was less successful, partly because Eisenhower delayed in forwarding some two hundred reports to Congress.

At the age of eighty-eight, nearly confined to a wheelchair and losing both his sight and his hearing, Hoover made one more trip to West Branch, Iowa, for the dedication of the Herbert Hoover Library. He was surprised and pleased to see that nearly 50,000 people had braved the blistering August heat to honor him.

Hoover died of colon cancer on October 20, 1964, at the age of ninety. Only one president, John Adams, had lived longer.

While many historians blame Herbert Hoover for the Great Depression, others view him as a president who embraced public service and problem solving.

Timeline

1874
Born August 10 in West Branch, Iowa

1891–1895
Attends Stanford University

1897
Hired by British firm Bewick, Moreing and Company; sent to goldfields of Australia

1899
Marries Lou Henry; travels to China to develop mines

1914
Heads the American Citizens' Relief Committee; organizes and directs the Commission for Relief in Belgium

1917
Serves as U.S. Food Administrator

1919
Directs the American Relief Administration

1870

1921–1929

Serves as secretary of commerce in the cabinets of Presidents Harding and Coolidge

1928

Elected thirty-first president

1932

Defeated in reelection bid by Franklin D. Roosevelt

1947

Serves as chairman of the Commission on Organization of the Executive Branch of the Government, known as the Hoover Commission

1953

Chairs the second Hoover Commission for President Eisenhower

1964

Dies in his New York hotel suite

1970

Notes

Chapter 1

p. 8, ". . . shared the 'common experience' . . .": Herbert Hoover, *The Memoirs of Herbert Hoover*, vol. 1, *Years of Adventure, 1874–1920*. New York: The Macmillan Company, 1951, p. 5.

p. 8, "'There was the swimming hole . . .'": "An Iowa Boyhood," Herbert Hoover Presidential Library and Museum, http://www.hoover.nara./ed (accessed 3/08).

p. 12, "'Turn your cheek once . . .'": Quoted in David Burner, *Herbert Hoover: A Public Life*. New York: Knopf, 1979, p. 19.

p. 12, "'Whatsoever thy hand findeth . . .'": Burner, p. 21.

p. 14, "'The Friends have always held . . .'": Hoover, *The Memoirs*, vol. 1, p. 8.

Chapter 2

p. 21, "'red dust, black flies, and white heat'": http://www.hoover.nara.gov/hooverbio.html (accessed 10/9/07).

p. 21, "'an even less successful creation . . .'": http://www.hoover.nara.gov/hooverbio.html (accessed 10/9/07).

p. 24, "'Will you marry me?'" Quoted in Burner, p. 32.

Chapter 3

p. 26, "'All [our] journeys were suddenly . . .'": Hoover, *The Memoirs*, vol. 1, p. 47.

p. 26, "'Late one evening . . .'": Hoover, *The Memoirs*, vol. 1, p. 51.

p. 29, "'I took my turn . . .'": Quoted in Burner, p. 37.

p. 30, "'Hoover was everywhere . . .'": Quoted in Burner, p. 37.

p. 31, "'I was then 27 . . .'": Quoted in http://www.hoover.nara.gov/education/hooverbio.html (accessed 10/9/07).

p. 36, "'His letters contain many references . . .'": Burner, p. 59.

p. 38, "'the slippery road of public life'": Hoover, *The Memoirs,* vol. 1, p. 148.

Chapter 4

p. 39, "'I did not realize it . . .'": Hoover, *The Memoirs*, vol. 1, p. 148.

p. 39, "'Many of them only wanted . . .'": Hoover, *The Memoirs*, vol. 1, p. 144.

p. 40, "'the greatest job Americans have undertaken . . .'": Quoted in Burner, p. 74.

p. 42, "'The Commission for Relief in Belgium is Hoover . . .'": Quoted in Burner, p. 90.

p. 43, "'Life is worth more, too . . .'": Quoted in http://www.hoover.nara.gov/hooverbio.html (accessed 10/9/07).

p. 47, "'The United States is not at war . . .'": Quoted in Burner, p. 127.

p. 47, "'Twenty million people are starving . . .'": Quoted in Burner, p. 130.

p. 49, "'I think he is precisely . . .'": Quoted in Gary Dean Best, *The Politics of American Individualism: Herbert Hoover in Transition, 1918-1921*. Westport, CT: University of Connecticut Press, 1975, p. 19.

CHAPTER 5

p. 52, "'It is the essence of this democracy . . .'": Quoted in Best, p. 19.

p. 60, "'. . . the greatest peace-time calamity . . .'": Quoted in Burner, p. 193.

p. 60, "'In the spring of 1927 . . .'": Burner, p. 193.

CHAPTER 6

p. 66, "'One hand is kept in his pocket . . .'": Quoted in Joan Hoff Wilson, *Herbert Hoover: Forgotten Progressive*. Boston: Little, Brown & Co., 1975, p. 28.

p. 69, "'My friends have made the American people . . .'": Quoted in Richard Norton Smith, *An Uncommon Man: The Triumph of Herbert Hoover*. Worland, WY: High Plains Publishing Co., Inc., 1984, p. 103.

p. 70, "'excessive fortunes are a menace . . .'": Quoted in Burner, p. 212.

p. 75, "'We in America today . . .'": Hoover's Acceptance Speech, August 1928, reproduced in "Oh Yeah: Herbert Hoover Predicts Prosperity": http://historymatters.gmu.edu/d/5063/ (accessed 4/30/08).

CHAPTER 7

p. 76, "'Stock prices virtually collapsed . . .'": "Stocks Collapse in 16,410,030-Share Day," *The New York Times*, Oct. 30, 1929. Reprinted in David A. Shannon, ed., *The Great Depression*, Englewood Cliffs, NJ: Prentice-Hall, Inc., 1960, p. 4.

p. 78, "'No one,'" he said, "'can measure . . .'": Quoted in "Roots of Disaster," in Ralph K. Andrist, ed., *The American Heritage History of the 20's & 30's*. New York: American Heritage Publishing Co., Inc., 1970, p. 178.

p. 80, "'Women office workers in New York . . .'": Quoted in David C. King et al., *The United States and Its People*, Menlo Park, CA: Addison-Wesley, 1995, p. 564.

p. 81, "'Gentlemen,'" he said, "'You have come . . .'": Quoted in Andrist, p. 181.

p. 81, "'During the spring of 1930 . . .'": Quoted in David C. King, et al, *The United States and Its People*, p. 566.

p. 83, "'The roads of the West and Southwest . . .'": from Committee on Labor Hearing, House of Representatives, 72nd Congress, U.S. Government Printing Office, 1932, quoted in David C. King, ed., *The Dust Bowl*, Carlisle, MA: Discovery Enterprises, Ltd., 1997, p. 17.

p. 85, "'We have come out of each previous depression . . .'": Quoted in Andrist, p. 178.

p. 86, "'Prosperity cannot be restored . . .'": Quoted in Andrist, p. 181.

p. 87, "'There was always a frown . . .'": Quoted in Andrist, p. 182.

p. 90, "'The major strategy of the opposition . . .'": Herbert Hoover, *The Memoirs of Herbert Hoover*, vol. 3, *The Great Depression, 1929–1941*. New York: The Macmillan Company, 1952, p. 218.

CHAPTER 8

p. 93, "'The use of the Atomic bomb . . .'": Quoted in Burner, p. 335.

GLOSSARY

American Citizens' Relief Committee committee set up by Herbert Hoover and others in 1914 to aid Americans stranded in England by the outbreak of World War I

American Relief Administration (ARA) agency established by the Wilson administration during World War I, and headed by Hoover, to help launch the rehabilitation of Europe

Commission for Relief in Belgium (CRB) commission that distributed an estimated 5 million tons of food to feed 7 million Belgians and 2 million French

blockade the isolation of a region achieved by controlling its coastline

buying on margin buying stocks with money borrowed from a stock broker

conservation in wartime, the effort to reduce the consumption of food, oil, and other goods required by the military

dole benefit paid by the government to the unemployed

dowager a widow with a title or property inherited from her late husband

Hooverizing a popular term for the voluntary conservation of food during World War I

individualism policy or philosophy that focuses on the individual

liberal political philosophy advocating greater individual freedoms

progressive similar to liberal; political philosophy advocating change and improvement

public works projects that help the general population; for example, the construction of highways, bridges, dams, and airports

Reconstruction Finance Corporation (RFC) agency established in 1932 by the Hoover administration to work for economic recovery

reparations payments for damages; Germany was forced to pay reparations after World War I

spheres of influence regions controlled by a government other than the legitimate one; a type of unofficial colony

standardization the practice of making things of the same type all have the same basic features so as to be interchangeable

Further Information

Books

Elish, Dan. *Franklin Delano Roosevelt*. New York: Marshall Cavendish Benchmark, 2009.

Landau, Elaine. *The Great Depression*. New York: Children's Press, 2007.

Venezia, Mike. *Herbert Hoover, Thirty-first President, 1929–1933*. New York: Children's Press, 2005.

DVD

The First World War. Image Entertainment, 2005.

Web Sites

Herbert Hoover Presidential Library and Museum

www.hoover.nara.gov

This site is dedicated to the nation's thirty-first president. Explore the exhibits and galleries of the museum to find information on Herbert Hoover.

Surviving the Dust Bowl

www.pbs.org/wgbh/amex/dustbowl/

Explore eyewitness accounts, government action, a timeline, and the people and events of the dust bowl.

BIBLIOGRAPHY

Andrist, Ralph K., ed. "Roots of Disaster" in *American Heritage History of the 20s and 30s*. New York: American Heritage Publishing Co., Inc., 1970.

Best, Gary Dean. *The Politics of American Individualism: Herbert Hoover in Transition, 1918–1921*. Westport, CT: University of Connecticut Press, 1975.

Burner, David. *Herbert Hoover: A Public Life*. New York: Knopf, 1979.

Fausold, Martin. *The Presidency of Herbert Hoover*. Kansas City: University of Kansas Press, 1984.

Hoover, Herbert. *The Memoirs of Herbert Hoover*, vol. 1, *Years of Adventure, 1874–1920*; vol. 2, *The Cabinet and the Presidency, 1920–1933*; vol. 3, *The Great Depression, 1929–1941*. New York: The Macmillan Co., 1951, 1952.

Robinson, Edgar Eugene, and Vaughn D. Bornet. *Herbert Hoover: President of the United States*. Stanford, CA: Hoover Institution Press, 1975.

Shannon, David A., ed. *The Great Depression*. Englewood Cliffs, NJ: Prentice-Hall, Inc., 1960.

Smith, Richard Norton. *An Uncommon Man: The Triumph of Herbert Hoover*. Worland, WY: High Plains Publishing Co. Inc., 1984.

Wilson, Joan Hoff. *Herbert Hoover: Forgotten Progressive*. Boston: Little, Brown & Co., 1975.

INDEX

Pages in **boldface** are illustrations.

★ ★

ABOUT THE AUTHOR

David C. King is an award-winning author of more than seventy books for readers aged ten to adult. Many of his books have been on topics from American history. King has also written a number of books in Marshall Cavendish's Cultures of the World series, including *Rwanda*, *Bosnia-Herzegovina*, *United Arab Emirates*, and *Greenland*. King and his wife, Sharon, live in New England's Berkshires, at the point where New York, Massachusetts, and Connecticut come together.